AN UNEASY PARADISE

LIVING ON THE WATERWAYS

By Sebastien & Louise

WANDERINGS
PUBLICATIONS

For all the people who relentlessly and tirelessly seek a vision of freedom that emanates from within themselves.

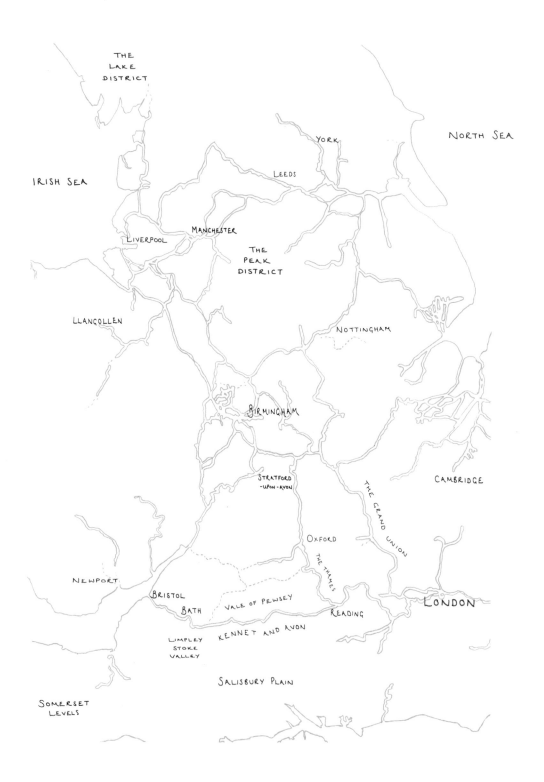

THE
LAKE
DISTRICT

NORTH SEA

IRISH SEA

YORK

LEEDS

LIVERPOOL

MANCHESTER

THE
PEAK
DISTRICT

LLANGOLLEN

NOTTINGHAM

BIRMINGHAM

STRATFORD
-UPON-AVON

CAMBRIDGE

THE GRAND UNION

OXFORD

THE THAMES

NEWPORT

BRISTOL

BATH

VALE OF PEWSEY

READING

LONDON

LIMPLEY
STOKE
VALLEY

KENNET AND AVON

SALISBURY PLAIN

SOMERSET
LEVELS

*T*he 18th century was an age of revolution and expansion; it was the age that gave birth to Napoleon, Wollstonecraft, Mozart and Turner. It was in this time, before the roads were tarmacked or the train lines were laid, that a large army of men, who came to be known as the navvies, began digging canals that would criss-cross the heart of Britain, connecting the rivers and the seas, the ports and the cities, to create an inland waterway system 4,800 miles long. Drawn by horse, narrowboats carried coal to the factories, wheat to the mills, and cotton to the looms, fuelling the boom that was to become the first Industrial Era; the era that uncoupled mankind from nature and turned Britain into the largest Empire the world had ever known.

Now, over two centuries later, these symbols of industry have a new role to play in what are once again fast-changing times. From the open vistas of the Pewsey Vale to the wooded hills of the Limpley Stoke Valley, a community has grown at the Western end of the Kennet and Avon Canal that is quite unlike any other; where as many as six hundred individuals, couples and families have chosen to make a boat their permanent home. Each independent of the others yet united by a stretch of water that shapes a communal identity, people of diverse ages and backgrounds have been drawn to this way of life by the beauty and freedom that it has to offer. Theirs is a nomadic existence, where nurses and architects, artists and teachers, have swapped convenience for nature, comfort for community, and discovered a lifestyle that affords them the simple pleasure of having a home of their own.

"At its best, photography is a symbol that not only serves to help illuminate some of the darkness of the unknown, but it also serves to lessen the fears that too often accompany the journeys from the known to the unknown."

Wynn Bullock

*E*arly morning in winter, the mist rises from the canal and the leaves glisten with their outlining of frost. The air is still and filled with silence. Nothing moves, only columns of smoke rising from soot-stained chimneys, a warm reminder that people are home and the routines of morning are beginning to stir.

"To find peace one must understand beauty, that is why it is important, while we are very young, to have beauty about us. In understanding what beauty is, we shall know love, for the understanding of beauty is the peace of the heart."

J. Krishnamurti

I started going onto the canal just before my eighth birthday, there was an old corrugated boathouse just behind my parent's house and one day an old boy said, "What you staring at, you want something to do? Clean out the boats and you can have a free go of one at the end of the day." And then I was just totally hooked.

When I was 15 I joined the Royal Navy and when I left in the later part of the 70s I volunteered on a steam dredger. The best way to describe it in my view was as a 'snorting dragon', it was absolutely beautiful, the noise, the hissing, the steam, the chugging and banging. Then in '91 a job came up for a lock-keeper with a beautiful house in the middle of nowhere looking after the deep cut flight of 14 locks on the Basingstoke Canal, and I was there 21 years.

In 2012 it was decided that a lock-keeper was no longer needed so that's when I bought my boat, *Grey Hare*, and I've been on it ever since; and though the canal has been a part of my life most of my life, it's the first boat I've actually owned.

– Peter

With the first warmth of spring, life spills onto the towpath and people begin, once again, to move further afield. To travel takes time and this is its delight; ancient and slow, moving through the locks the rhythm is set by the pace of the water and the mind must adjust to its flow.

I love the change of the seasons, I love it when it's changing, even in the winter when all of a sudden it starts snowing, when all of a sudden the sun comes out, or when all of a sudden there's a storm. I love the change of season when all of a sudden the leaves are falling or when the buds are coming out after winter, I love that.

– Luca

I moved onto the canal about five years ago. I'd been walking along the towpaths around here for many years before I got my boat, always thinking I would like to have one of my own one day and live on the water, and that window of opportunity came to me when my eldest child left home and my youngest was very keen to move onto the canal as well.

Living this way has simplified my life; I swim a lot in the river and live more naturally and harmoniously with nature. It makes me feel more in tune with everything and not be too separate and wrapped up in a human-dominating world where people believe they're superior to nature and that they can conquer it.

The longer I am here the more I feel a sense of belonging. The community here welcomed me, but like any community it has its ups and downs and its difficulties, it's not perfect anymore than any other community or world. It's not idyllic. There's a lot of hard work, there's conflict as well as joys. I think that it reflects the truth about the state of the world and so maybe it is more honest.

This way of life has completely changed my mindset, which is perhaps the most important of all. The way I am about everything, my whole thinking, has completely altered. The moving is refreshing and stops the stagnation and now I feel I've got to a point of no return, I don't think I could live in a house-type dwelling again.

– Julia

I'm proud to be the coalman. How unique in this world is this daily experience? There are maybe 35 of us in the whole of England doing this job, and there's only one of me on this canal. It's a very magical and honourable thing to have all of these people trusting you. When you become a coalman you have a feeling that you are part of history, you are part of that tradition, you are part of the reason why the canals were built. On a busy run I can load six to eight tonnes of coal, that's a lot of coal to a lot of people.

The coal boat's 70ft, my cabin is 24ft and the rest is just cargo – coal, gas, diesel, kindling, etc. That's it, I have somewhere to sleep, somewhere to sit, somewhere to clean myself and my clothes, and somewhere to cook, and they're the fundamental things in accommodation, aren't they? You need those and it's home. My whole life is on this canal, there are few things I need from out there, here's my reality. I open my back door and I'm at work, there's no rush hour, there's no hassle, there's no shirt and tie, it's just sun goes up sun goes down, I love it. Part of the responsibility of the coalman, I believe, is to be part of the community, have cups of tea with people, make friends, be nice, happy and chirpy; if there's ice on the ground and someone's fallen on hard times and can't heat their boat let them have a bag or two of coal, I know that eventually I'll get my money back, well, at least most of it! With the boat always in perpetual motion, how free you become. You're not tied, and that's lovely. Everyday is something different, there are so many privileges – I feel privileged and honoured to be able to do this job, to serve a community and hopefully succeed to a certain degree.

– Will

Go Wi Flow was a character. She was more than the metal and wood that made her. She was my companion. I was always happy to see her when I headed home along the towpath, through the mud or with the sun on my back. After I bought her in Lancashire, it took me six weeks to cruise her down to the Kennet and Avon, and I spent a lot of that journey on my own. It was a time in my life when I was emerging from some darkness and uncertainty and finding my feet again. There were many breakdowns and mishaps as we cruised rivers and locks with *Flow*'s little outboard engine stuttering along. Much of it felt very sweet, and the way was full of the subtle coincidences and magic that I've only found on the canal side. I had a desk built in over the bed, and shelves wherever they would fit for my books. She was my creative hideaway and then my home. I fell in love on that boat, with the stove blazing and beeswax candles turning everything gold. She held me through a lot of despair and grief too, like a kingfisher's nest, so safe and secret. A part of my heart will always be with that little tin can of a narrowboat.

– Sophie

I think a big part of living this way is having peace away from technology. I had quite a bad technology addiction before I lived on a boat, I was video gaming eight to 10 hours a day and I didn't have the self control, or the willpower, to stop in that environment because essentially I wasn't happy. I was doing a job I didn't like and I was paying so much for my rent, so I was trying to sort of supplement happiness and adventure by playing video games.

I remember sleeping on the boat the first night, I was looking through the porthole window at the full moon, the light was shinning onto me and I was lying there thinking 'this is beautiful, this is amazing' – I could move my boat, I could adventure whenever I wanted and I didn't need technology to do that. The world that night became full of opportunities, it became bigger and more exciting than any open-world computer game could ever be.

– Liem

*L*ong days and late nights,
summer cycles in the moonlight.

"Freedom is not merely a right but a skill to be acquired, the skill to view the world through different lenses, through lenses other than one's own, the skill to imagine what no-one has imagined before, to find beauty or meaning or inspiration. Each life is a fable about freedom."

Theodore Zeldin

I was on my way to Brighton with my bag on my back to go and share a room with a friend and find a job, I'd just graduated from my sociology degree, which just kind of catapulted me into the open world. At university you live in this bubble – you have your loan, you have your money, you know what you're doing with your time, you feel set up in where you're at – then following that it was like *what now?* I've got to find money to pay rent every month and figure out what I'm going to do with my life. On the way I visited a friend who lived on a boat and I fell in love with the way of life instantly. It was like heaven at the time. I didn't know much about canals before, I just presumed if you wanted to live on the canal you'd have to have quite an expensive boat, I didn't know that there were many options. That day I was shown a boat for sale that was financially possible and I could pay in monthly instalments, I literally bought it two days later, I had my bag already with me and that was it, little gypsy boat became my home for just over a year.

This time really gave me a sense of community, which I really needed at that point in my life. It gave me that space to really tune into what I wanted and it helped me to express myself and gave me a foundation. You didn't have to pay lots of rent so I didn't have to work full-time and I was able to nurture myself and my spirit. It gave me confidence and connected me back with nature. In a sense, it actually gave me hope. A hope that it is possible to find a community and connection, connection to each other, and connection to nature. It's definitely been a vital stepping-stone in my life to where I am now.

– Francesca

*T*he moment you step onto the towpath you are enveloped into a world that you know is always your own. A place aside, away from the frenetic world beyond. Here along the long line of the towpath, for now at least, there are many who know they are at home.

I'd just finished university in Bath where I'd studied fine-art painting. I had a friend at the time who lived on the canal, and that's what inspired me. I thought if I lived on a boat then I wouldn't have to work as much, and I could spend that time creating and focusing on my own pursuits.

I only had £6,000 and that won't buy you much in terms of a narrowboat, so I arrived at the idea of buying a lifeboat. I started by looking at ship-breakers from all around the world, then one day I decided to do a search on eBay and found a guy selling a totally enclosed lifeboat in Wales. It was only two hours away so I went there the next day. But for a wood-burning stove he'd put in, it was totally unconverted. Originally it had been on a gas platform and it still had all the seats for 66 people, as well as water rations and stuff in little packets that were fifteen years out of date.

The winter I moved on was one of the worst winters we had had for many years. There was no insulation on the boat, all I had was the stove, and all the condensation on the inside was freezing up. I had a cat at the time called Danny; I would go to bed with as many layers on as I could and the cat would get into bed with me, but in the end it got so cold that Danny couldn't handle it anymore and moved to the boat next door. I had the boat for six years, slowly upgrading it so that it was more functional. I learnt a lot living that way. I could never have anticipated the feeling of connection to the land, and to the seasons, that the hardship of basic living would bring.

– Lewin

I get quite an overwhelming sense of being at home when I'm on the boat, when I'm just sitting on the deck looking into the trees, that is home for me – just a safe place, where you belong, where you feel comfortable.

I think a lot of people forget, or don't realise, that these are people's homes. It can seem funny when you walk past because they all look so small, but in there there's a whole world – there are beds for everybody and that's where everybody has their breakfast. I can imagine if you're not used to it, and you haven't visited one, you don't realise that it looks smaller from the outside than it is on the inside, you know a bit like a Tardis. I think once you're in you understand that actually you've got everything you need.

– Annie

"Peace is not an idea opposed to war. Peace is a way of life, for there can be peace only when everyday life is understood."

J. Krishnamurti

On the canal everyone comes together and everyone provides something different, we've all kind of stumbled across this and then we all add to it, we all participate. I think it's good that our community is colourful and distinctive; I think we should celebrate our diversity and how different our lifestyle is.

It's wonderful, the whole boating life. Here life is really simple. People aren't always rushing around. I feel secure. I know all of my neighbours and everyone is looking out for each other. I have this lovely community and I feel blessed I've made such good life choices. On the canal I'm never bored because I'm surrounded by beauty – I can look out my window and watch the ravens courting or the barn owl hunting. We make our own entertainment; we play music, we have fires, we forage, and it's all absolutely free. During lockdown I wanted for nothing. I didn't need to buy anything, or get anything, or change my life in any way. I've realised that everything that actually makes me truly happy are the things we've evolved with; sitting round a fire or having a swim in the river, being in a community, these make me feel satisfied in a way that money can't. I think we're very lucky, here on the canal, that so many of us feel satisfied with comparatively little.

– Becky

*A*s the air cools and the evenings draw in, and the fallen leaves float lazily on the water, thoughts turn inwards as lives move indoors, and playful summer days seem a long time past.

Yeah, it was always just a shed.

When I met Gem I was living in Manchester. I had a flat full of stuff, you know like tools and stuff, I'd lived there all my life and she was on a 53ft working boat. I had a bit of money saved, so I started looking at old workboats and found this one on Apollo Duck. I got a load of timber and built the front out of that and then we just towed it around.

I have thought a bit about living in a house recently because we have started living the normal life so to speak, you know, school run, work, blah blah blah. But then it's like 'same place everyday' you know what I mean, it's the same, and it's the community, isn't it? We went to Toronto for a week and I just remember when we got back the walk from getting out the car to the boat, I don't know how many people I saw, but it was like loads of just little chats – chit chat, chit chat – I enjoyed that little bit more than the previous week.

– Kev

Woodpiles stacked and chimney flues swept, a sun with no heat awaits the mythical whiteness of winter.

This morning I walked the mile or so to the library along the towpath, the sky was a perfect blue and the light in the trees caught all the brightness of the small birds that they house. The puddles were frozen as too was the canal, and all about was a perfect stillness bathed in a golden light.

In spite of the cold, people were out, and in spite of having things to do, everyone had time to say hello. A boater I'd not met before greeted me with a warm good morning that led to a conversation about all number of things; a familiar face appeared on a bicycle with time to stop and quickly catch up to make sure all was well; another opened a window with a cheery wave and a joyful smile, and I felt blessed to live amongst so many kindly faces in a world where loneliness causes so much pain.

– Louise

"If the rose at noon has lost the beauty it had at dawn, the beauty it had then was real. Nothing in the world is permanent and we're foolish when we ask for anything to last. But surely we're still more foolish not to take delight in it while we have it."

W. Somerset Maugham

"If you care about something you have to protect it – If you're lucky enough to find a way of life you love, you have to find the courage to live it."

John Irving

AN UNEASY PARADISE

By Sebastien and Louise

Through the eyes of a traveller, a grey winter's day becomes full of subtle shades of green and brown, and the commonplace soon becomes humorous or absurd, and so it was with England. After eight years in Asia, years in which we had taken tea with Himalayan kings and celebrated festivals with hunter-gatherers; spent nights out at sea with fishermen and been silenced by the beauty of Hindu temples, it was time to return home, but not to settle, to explore – March 2012

The chapter in our lives that sees us moving on to a narrowboat is part of a much greater story that began many years earlier in Northern Thailand, where we lay sweltering in the blistering heat awaiting visas that would permit us re-entry into India. It was the beginning of an idea; somewhere to escape to in our imaginations; a seed that would slowly take root. For many years we had been more at home in Asia than in England and this deep love was to continue for many years more, but in the early summer of 2009, hot and tired, the first cracks in the romance were beginning to show.

To us, the beauty of travel is to see the world for oneself, for we believe each person holds their own truth, and we did not want ours to be led or shaped by the highly-orchestrated, commercial forces of any particular cultural authority. The world that we had set out to discover so many years before was changing fast, and with it, we found ourselves moving ever faster, and with ever greater urgency, to bear witness to the unique ways people, communities and cultures lived and survived. We had wanted to see unpolluted rivers and walk in virgin forests, to see a world populated by local traditions, customs and clothing, and to see, if only for a moment, what existed before a planet homogenised by a handful of multinational corporations – a world that is becoming inhabited by a monoculture of human personality, ironically centred around individualism[1]. We wanted to bear witness to a free people; free in the sense of a person's ability to act, think, and develop without being dominated by unaccountable figures, and institutions[2].

We went looking to experience other ways of thinking, to try to learn from and understand not only other cultures and their histories, but also the evolution of the stories that have come to shape and dominate the views, ways and purposes of the Industrialised West; the stories that have taken humanity from nomadic hunter-gatherers, to sedentary sitters, encapsulated in modern glass towers. We were seeking to understand the evolution of religions – to understand the animists, to bear witness to the true belief a person can hold in an elephant-headed god. Yet over our years of travel it became increasingly hard to ignore the speed at which marketed globalisation was spreading, and how, with incredible ferocity, it was coming to dominate more and more of the places that had inspired us, as they fell prey to a singular globalised image. (An image peddled by corporate interests, pushing the values of materialism, a system "preoccupied with possessions and the social image they project[3]".) Litter, debt, depression and anxiety[4] – all the by-products of humanity's insatiable, yet highly manipulated, addiction to consumption were transforming the lives and landscapes of those we knew.

We watched countless hotels building swimming pools, and industries diverting water sources, at a time when water levels had dropped so low that families who relied on subsistence farming could no longer grow crops. We saw locally-produced products, most often packaged in leaves or reusable containers, being replaced with highly-branded multinational ones that could be neither recycled nor reused. We observed the effect of repeated exposure to images of luxury goods and idealised Western lifestyles as televisions (that when we first began our travels were only just becoming affordable) entered every home. And we witnessed rich and vibrant cultures choke, and their communities erode, as the psychological and technological capabilities of advertisers

---

1 Matthew Crawford, *The World Beyond Your Head: How to Flourish in an Age of Distraction,* (London: Viking, 2014), p.17

2 Standing, Guy. *Basic Income: And How We Can Make It Happen,* (London: Pelican Books, 2017), p. 58

3 Monbiot, George. 'Materialism: a system that eats us from the inside out', *The Guardian,* 9th December 2013

4 "A series of studies published in the journal Motivation and Emotion in July showed that as people become more materialistic, their wellbeing (good relationships, autonomy, sense of purpose and the rest) diminishes. As they become less materialistic, it rises." See Monbiot, George. 'Materialism: a system that eats us from the inside out', *The Guardian,* 9th December 2013

became ever more far-reaching; their messages, which cast people as consumers rather than citizens, creating a system of expectations and preferences that led to desiring foreign commodities over domestic ones[5]. Yet when we returned to England and discussed our concerns with family and friends, a common opinion was that this process should not be questioned, as it is unjust to deny others what the Western world has already got.

* * *

"Our unreflective and obsessive pursuit of banal material well-being and status is abhorrent. Where does a society go that no longer reflects on where it is going?"

Andrew Smart

What is it that the 'Western world' has 'got', and what makes its people believe so determinably in its correctness? For those whose only experience of Western culture has been through television and advertising, it appears to be perceived as a place of affluence and abundance. On numerous occasions in Asia we were met with an overwhelming disbelief when we spoke of homelessness or unemployment in the UK. At home and abroad, the media presents the Western world as a place of superior monetary wealth, where shopping for non-essential items is a national pastime and individuals are able to fly all over the world taking holidays for pleasure. This image inspires an aspirational desire for a lifestyle that is idealised and neglects to consider its consequences.

In Asia we had lived for long periods amongst people of limited material wealth, whose strong foundations of community and family afforded a life of satisfaction, without being overwhelmed by agonising want. Yet as the grips of commercialism took hold, we watched this world change. The first wave brought great joy, as each and every family attained new levels of domestic comfort – large glazed windows brought heat and light into mountain homes; a shoebox size water turbine brought a light bulb into the bamboo house of a family of hunter-gatherers;

---

5 "When India began opening up its economy and American corporations were able to really start moving in, the first domain they took over was advertising. Very quickly, Indian advertising agencies became subsidiaries of big foreign ones, mostly based in the US." See Chomsky, Noam. *How the World Works,* (London: Hamish Hamilton, 2012), p. 251

an electric pump brought running water into the kitchen of a family of fishermen.

But further down the line, once comforts had been met and consumers had been created, the impact of the next wave had more dubious results. With increased advertising came unrealistic comparisons, and successful mountain communities became ghost towns as the young sought their fortunes in cities, having begun to consider themselves poor for the first time. Alcoholism destroyed families as its heavy promotion in a culture, where it had long been absent, proved too much to contend with. And unchecked, large-scale commercial fishing for an ever-growing market, emptied the coastal waters of life, leaving traditional fishermen, once proud of their profession, completely destitute as their livelihood vanished.

* * *

"Nothing is enough for the man whom enough is too little."

Epicurus

There is no denying that over the last century there has been an impressive and unprecedented period of economic growth on the planet. Yet it must not be forgotten that this impressive development has been primarily fuelled by natural resources, and that this model of economic growth continues to be largely based on excess. Much that has led to this growth, simply cannot work today – almost certainly not in any given region; certainly not at a planetary level. The natural reserves are quickly depleting. That's not only the oil, gas and coal, but also fresh water and phosphorous, an element without which plants cannot grow. It is a commonly-quoted concept (based on the infographic illustrations of science writer Tim De Chant[6]) that if everyone on the globe was to consume as much, and produce as much waste as the West, then three planets would be needed to support the global population.

Furthermore, a collective desire for individual gain over collective good, coupled with a self-serving materialism that has come to be accepted as legitimate, even praiseworthy, in which celebrity culture and capitalism have become inextricably intertwined, is

---

6 McDonald, Charlotte. 'How many earths do we need?', *BBC News Magazine,* 16th June 2015

producing a culture of unlimited expectations and subsequent debt[7]. That the significance of ordinary life is largely ignored, whilst extravagant material wealth is idealised rather than denigrated by the silent majority; that the vocal minority's veneration of short-termist financial success could come at the expense of the human species' long-term survival (and already comes daily at the expense of other species), is both a tragedy and a farce.

The people of the world have to face up to the inevitable consequences of the model that has been so singularly promoted, and ask themselves, do they have the capability to surpass the negative outcomes of a system that potentially has so much to offer? To further understand this, and the phenomenon that was enveloping Asia, we felt a need to return to England. We wanted to see this model in the environment in which it had first begun, and pay conscious attention to the outcome it was having on its own land and people. We wanted to discover whether those who had lived with the benefits and distractions of this way of life the longest were coming up with solutions to overcome the difficulties that it had created. We needed to find hope; to find living examples of positive models for the future – ones in which people can pursue sustainable, creative and fulfilling ways of being; ones that the global majority, not just its most infamous minority, find accessible.

Upon our return we sought to find a people bored with the cheap entertainments and unachievable illusions, and discover a creative and engaged few that would be reclaiming their time and their imagination. Onto this land we had pinned our hopes of encountering narratives being fought out, directed at a more rewarding and sustainable society, one in which community values are rendered paramount, and minds can be engaged in proactive and positive solutions, rather than subdued and blunted by fear and hopelessness. If, as Iris Murdoch said, "man is the animal that makes pictures of himself, and then comes to resemble the pictures" then humanity needs to start creating better pictures of itself, ones that offer a *positive* image – an image weighed not against levels of consumption, material wealth and vanity, but against active compassion, intelligent adaptability and the preservation of the planet.

---

7 The average UK household owes £15,385, not counting their mortgages, see Toynbee, Polly and Walker, David. 'The lost decade: the hidden story of how austerity broke Britain', *The Guardian*, 3rd March 2020

*　*　*

"Let us learn from the past to profit by the present, and from the present,
to live better in the future."
William Wordsworth

18th century Britain was the birthplace of the Industrial Revolution, where a profound escalation of inventive engineering and geo-political ambition afforded the nation temporary world domination. It also saw the rise of the world's first aggressive multinational corporation, the British East India Company, a business that by the 1750s, was already operating at an unprecedented scale, and which would eventually grow to become the most advanced capitalist organisation in the world[8] – a proto-corporation of sorts whose 'win at all costs' agenda foretells (albeit less subtly) the modus operandi of the current global market, where estimates suggest that half the world's largest economies are now multinational corporations[9].

It was an age of steam, canals and factories; it was an age that would change the face of Britain and the world forever. The advancements of the period brought new techniques and technologies into agriculture, substantially increasing the yield of saleable food yet reducing the human labour required to grow and harvest it. This, in conjunction with the escalation of land enclosures[10], led to severe unemployment and rising poverty in many rural areas, forcing many to leave the countryside in search of work in towns and cities. The world stage – with its spotlight on Britain – was set for a large-scale, city-based, labour-intensive factory system; a system whose own technological advances were marshalled around concepts concerning collective identity,

8 Dalrymple, William. *The Anarchy: The Relentless Rise of the East India Company,* (London: Bloomsbury Publishing, 2019), p. xxxi
9 Wilkinson, Richard and Pickett, Kate. *The Spirit Level: Why Equality is Better for Everyone,* (London: Penguin, 2010), p. 244
10 Between 1604 and 1914 6.8 million acres of common land was enclosed, systematically taking it away from the ordinary people. See Smith, P. D. 'Who owns England? By Guy Shrubsole review - our darkest secret', *The Guardian,* 10th May 2019

and augmented by philosophies prone to denigrating the virtues of personal freedom[11].

Transportation was key to the growth of these booming industries, along with the rapidly-expanding centres of population that accompanied them; and so began the construction of a network of canals that by 1850, connected over 4,800 miles of inland waterways, carrying thousands of tonnes of raw materials and manufacturing goods. The canals were at the heart of the industrial era, connecting all of Britain's largest and most prominent towns, cities and ports, and their very legacy would provide us with a most engaging and unique way to explore the country's industrial past and gain insight into its present-day transformation.

* * *

"Travel is at its most rewarding when it ceases to be about your reaching a destination and becomes indistinguishable from living your life."

Paul Theroux

Every journey we have embarked on is a search for beauty, and every place holds its joys and its sadnesses. The joy of travel is in the unexpected beauty, the beauty of the people, the culture and the landscape. It is also in the way one travels. The slow steady plod of the pack mule, the gentle rattle of an Indian train, these experiences are never forgotten, and for this journey, no way of travel could have been more fitting or appropriate than a 58ft narrowboat.

The canals had been part of our consciousness since childhood. We had both grown up in Bath, and had taken many walks along the towpath of the Kennet and Avon. But it was not until years later, sheltering from the midday heat in a high-rise hotel in Chiang Mai, the fan laying dormant due to power failure, when we began fantasising about cooler climes and a place of our own, that the dream of a narrowboat began to grow. We were excited for early June dawns and misty September mornings, for rainy days by the fire and

---

11 See Graeber, David. *Bullshit Jobs: A Theory*, (London: Simon and Schuster, 2019), for details about the psychological and practical effects of time clocks entering factories; the changes to education that were self-consciously designed to train children for lives of factory labour; and the origins, in slave plantations and on merchant ships, of modern work discipline and capitalist techniques of supervision that were imposed on the working poor.

crystal frosts in the trees, and all this a most beautiful backdrop to a way of life that we had caught glimpses of on our many walks along the canal. We began to dream that one day this way of life could be ours, and that when that day would come, the dream and the reality would be as one. A narrowboat would simultaneously fulfil our need for transport and our yearning for a home; a home without the requirement to settle. No more visa runs, no more living out of a backpack. It would be that place of our own, self-contained, with all that we needed, offering us a 'beauty in transit' no other form of transport could provide.

Always at home yet always on the move, when travelling by canal you're somewhat more than a visitor staying in a B&B. You become, for a moment, part of the community. You see the country change slowly and almost imperceptibly, as the canals wind through miles of green countryside, taking you through hamlets rarely visited by outsiders, or through the heart of England's major cities. Travelling by canal we would be able to stop anywhere at anytime, and would be afforded the privilege of exploring at our own speed. A million miles away from the dull grey tarmac of the road, the canals would provide us with a unique opportunity to feel at once close to nature and physically present in an historical past.

* * *

"No person, I think, ever saw a herd of buffalo, of which a few were fat and the great majority lean. No person ever saw a flock of birds, of which two or three were swimming in grease, and the other all skin and bone."

Henry George

On our return from Asia, our first purchase was of an up-to-date map of the waterways that confirmed, to our great delight, that the vast majority of the network, despite its abandonment and neglect over the previous century, was now largely restored and navigable. Our next challenge was to search for a boat that could accommodate a photographic darkroom – granted, a very specific requirement. But much to our surprise, just 20 miles from our hometown, there she was. After a winter of sandpaper and paint we were ready to go. *Mrs Macaw* was no longer red and grey, she was blue and yellow. Inside she had become our home; outside she would be a floating photography gallery, enabling us to sell our prints as we moved.

At a speed never much faster than walking pace we spent over a year and a half travelling through England on these waterways, from Bath to Liverpool and back – through its villages, its hamlets, its gridded cites and its dormitory towns. We travelled over and around its pristine green hills. We saw the old potteries, chocolate factories and industrial ruins. We pulled and pushed our narrowboat through countless locks and swing bridges, all with the accompanying background hum of the engine. And what we witnessed was a country divided. We would moor in towns where all the shops in the high street were boarded up, alcoholism and drug abuse was prominent, and a sense of foreboding danger and depravity hung in the air, (a far cry from the images of luxury and indulgence of the advertisements glued onto the buses and billboards around the town). A mile or so further along, the canal would see us back out to pristine hills, with country houses carved gently into the landscape – reminders of Britain's colonial past, their acres of private land once the quiet reserves of the gentry and the rich, now increasingly owned by the National Trust and international buyers. And let us not forget the immaculate villages of second homes, devoid of life, seldom inhabited, but kept preserved and intact as prime assets: status reminders of individual success.

We were surprised at the contrast of England's poverty and immense wealth, but in both we felt a stifling stagnation, fuelled as they were by an overwhelming lack of imagination and conservatism. The vast wealth of the country appeared to be concentrated in the hands of too few, and the youth, who had not left for larger cities, were left with very little prospects.

We were disappointed, but this was hard to admit. For years we had wondered about the state of England but never imagined that it would be so uninspiring. For years we had dreamt of our time travelling between canal communities (like the one glimpsed so close to home), not realising that it was in fact, a very localised phenomenon. Days would pass when only a handful of boats were seen, and these were mostly made up of a tight demographic of older boat owners that looked down disparagingly upon those of us who used our boats as a home. We listened to tales of the community that had once existed on the South Oxford Canal and how it was dispersed. And we watched as moorings on the Grand Union and in London where removed, privatised, or sold off in auction, causing congestion and conflict upon the limited mooring spaces remaining. Our hopes felt in vain. We saw neither flicker of hope nor shadow of change. Instead we saw a country living under a cloak of fear, distraction and resignation. And though we sought refuge in the beauty of nature and told ourselves it was all part of the learning process, we returned to the Kennet and Avon Canal with heavy hearts.

* * *

"We shall not cease from exploration
And the end of all our exploring
Will be to arrive where we started
And know the place for the first time."

T. S. Eliot

Two hundred and seventy years after the first canals were built to fuel an ever-demanding Empire, at the western edges of the Kennet and Avon Canal, a community had grown quite unlike any other. At any given time there can be as many as 600 boats[12] serving as homes to a community of nomadic boat dwellers, artists, gardeners, health-care workers, shop assistants, activists, professors, bakers, welders, rope sellers, architects, and independent thinkers, inextricably bound by a dark muddy stretch of water. People who have temporarily managed to create an existence for themselves outside of the constraints of mainstream society, where they have found truly affordable homes, ones that do not require a lifetime of debt to pay off. A group that have found a shared way to live beyond the metropolis, surrounded by nature, constructing lives for themselves lived in tune with the seasons. It is our belief that a life lived close to nature permits a person to harmonise their time with the rhythms of their landscape, stilling the mind and creating a greater respect for the planet and its resources. But so few young people grow up amongst the birds and the trees, the land and the rivers; so few are taught to *appreciate* these wonders, they can hardly

---

12 There are no accurate statistics of how many people live on boats. The Wiltshire Council 2017 Boaters Survey, published in May 2018, estimates that there are approximately 500 boats used for residential purposes in Wiltshire. There are no such statistics for Bath and North East Somerset. The Kennet and Avon Boating Community Interim Report, published in 2011, estimated that there were 175 boats without a mooring between Devizes and Bath. If half of these were in BANES, and an allowance is made for the increase in numbers over nine years, we consider 600 boats, serving as homes at the Western end of the Kennet and Avon Canal to be a reasonable estimate.

be expected to understand or care for them. For it is only with love and understanding, a comprehensive comprehension, that everything, indeed *anything*, will be saved.

The people of the Kennet and Avon Canal community have managed to carve out a way of life for themselves that has allowed them to reinvent their relationship with society. They have discovered a way to reclaim their time and their thoughts. In so doing, they have found the means to raise their families with beliefs closer to their own hearts and minds than might otherwise be the case were they forced, in the absence of community, or in the necessity to support a less affordable lifestyle, to rely on nursery care from infancy and afterschool care through childhood. It is a community where, for the most part, quality of life takes precedence over quantity of consumption and where people have a tangible connection with the resources they consume. Theirs is an intelligent and conscious community, a conscientiously composed community, that has actualised for itself the gift of time, and we were grateful for the privilege of being able to join this group.

* * *

"When you feel that you are not being compelled to do anything, you will find out what you are interested in, and then for the rest of your life you will do something which you really love to do."

J. Krishnamurti

A boat is a way of regaining a community whilst retaining autonomy; a community comprised of a supportive network of individuals that are able to choose their neighbours and times of solitude. It is a place to think and create, without the constant impact of advertising, or other societal pressures to conform. Constantly in motion yet united by a stretch of water, through shared experience and shared hardships, canal dwellers have formed networks of friendships that bind them together and hold them to a place that when seen through open eyes, is blessed with a touch of magic.

The only rule that must be followed (for licensing purposes) is that boats without a home mooring should not remain in any one location for longer than two weeks, and though to some this may seem unsettling, there's an excitement and a beauty to moving that encapsulates the essence of what it is to live on a boat. On moving day, the whole family packs up and settles again in a new but familiar spot, routines change, the mind freshens, and life continues with a new set of friends as neighbours, and neighbours as friends. This hardy, but hardly complex, process replenishes both the community as a whole and in parts, and the individual as a part of the whole. One can feel it giving a freedom to the spirit and courage to the soul.

Inherent in the boat community's lifestyle is a reduced impact on the environment that goes beyond a preference for cycling. Our very first evening moored up on the towpath taught us that much. We recall our amazement that detached from the land and surrounded by water, we were able to cook on a gas hob and read a book by electric light. The realisation that all of our needs were contained within this long metal tube quickly transformed into an intense awareness of exactly what these needs were. Our gas, our water, our electricity, our fuel to heat the boat, all were physically measurable. We became more aware than ever before that what we take from the earth deserves monitoring. The need to adjust our behaviour where necessary had become immediately apparent.

In the summer our electricity is provided exclusively by solar panels, and in the winter it can be topped up with the help of the engine. But regardless of how it is created, the capacity for storage is limited to the size and number of the batteries. The limiting of this resource forces you to think more carefully about how you use it: you cannot while away hours in front of the television, or any other devices, thus minimising the absorption of intrusive advertising and detrimental messages of violence (every year the average person sees 2,600 murders on their screens[13] and every day in excess of 5,000 advertisements[14]), but you can find moments in which your mind has time to rest and explore its own imagination, as well as plentiful opportunities to read a book or play an instrument, to draw, or talk, or to go for a walk. In essence, on a boat one has far greater control over the wanderings of one's mind and its focus of attention. By turning off these screens so much *time* is created: time free from the prescribed influences of what one *should* do, and who one *should* be. (Not to mention *what one next should buy*.)

---

13 Dalai Lama. *A Call for Revolution*, (London: Rider, 2017), p. 48
14 https://airoutdoor.co.uk/blog/how-many-ads-seen-one-day/

Thanks to the fewer working hours required to support a more modest lifestyle, time becomes one of the most treasured elements of life for those who live on the waterways.

It is our belief that interactions between people are the backbone of human existence and an essential component in the creation of any healthy society, and along the towpath conversation is granted its proper value as an important use of time. It is also a unique feature of the boating community that it is open to anyone – there are no committees that grant acceptance, or waiting lists where it helps to know someone to be granted preference – and this has facilitated its becoming a community of diverse ages, occupations and social backgrounds. When we moved aboard our narrowboat in 2012, we knew nobody, but we were welcomed instantly with offers of help should we need it, and a great many hot cups of tea. Very quickly we felt that we were part of something special.

The friendships that we formed in those early days have stayed with us, and the importance of these connections became particularly apparent to us recently when our son was born. The help and support, sometimes simply the reassurance that such a network of families existed, made this transition in our lives a joyous and fearless one, free from the feelings of isolation or helplessness so many suffer. Connections between families are essential for a successful society because through them people feel supported, not isolated, and are able to create the strong foundations the children that grow between them will need. Loneliness is combated through close community, and, in this semi-nomadic environment, movement actually refreshes relationships, so that patterns of life that distance people from one another are (somewhat ironically) *less* likely to form.

For those who are unfamiliar with this lifestyle, closer inspection will reveal a group of people whose homes may be a different shape and their clothes a different style to their own, but whose routines will look remarkably similar. People on boats get up in the morning to go to work, and parents take children to school, cook dinners for them and uphold bedtimes just as they would in any other part of England. To be a part of the boating community is not to opt out of society, but to opt into an ideal that still holds dear many of the values that are lamentably being lost in wider social circles. Neighbourliness, kindliness and a willingness to give help; these we believe are the foundations of a strong and beautiful way of life. Many people will not stay for long, a couple of years on their journey to whatever comes next, but the exchange of ideas that takes place in this space helps to form important patterns for the future. For to live amongst, or even to bear witness with an open mind, to a people living with a freedom of spirit, can fuel the imagination with possibilities and hopes that have the power to last a lifetime.

* * *

"It is our ethnic and cultural diversity – our differences in language, customs and beliefs – that provide the strength, resiliency and creativity of our species."
Octavio Paz

The community that can be seen living on the Kennet and Avon today is the latest chapter in a long history of families settling on the waterways. Just half a century after the first canal had been completed the first train lines arrived, and the competition this created forced carrying companies on the canals to reduce their wages. In turn boatmen had no choice but to move their families out of their homes and onto their boats, making a permanent life for themselves on board[15]. By the mid 1800s, floating communities had become firmly established across the country with a lifestyle and culture of their very own, (the inherent unenforceability of their marginalised existence giving them an unusual element of freedom in a closed Victorian society[16]). However, as the social reforms of the 19th century began to take hold, campaigners cast their efforts in the direction of the canal. They painted a portrait, published and circulated by church organisations and serialised in magazines, of a filthy and immoral community – one that was considered less than human; one that for its lack of church attendance was condemned as dirty, illiterate and godless[17].

By the 1960s, canal haulage had dramatically declined and the last of the generations of traditional canal families were moving off, but it was not long before they were replaced by a new group of boat owners. Throughout the 1970s, narrowboats could be bought and restored cheaply, and a new generation emerged attracted by the alternative lifestyle and the possibility of being able to own their own home, one that

15 McIvor, Liz. *Canals: The Making of a Nation*, (London: BBC Books, 2015), p. 209
16 Ibid, p. 211
17 Ibid, pp. 225-234

was economical to run[18]. It is estimated that approximately 11,000 boats are now lived on permanently in the UK, one third of the total number of boats on the water[19], and of these, 5,500 are registered as continuous cruisers (boaters without a home mooring). Yet the stigma generated in the 19th century has survived into the 21st, and boating communities today continue to be regarded by many with mistrust. Sadly, throughout our years on the canal we have encountered first-hand, or have had recounted to us, numerous instances of long-established prejudices still held against boat people.

A great many times, both on our travels around the country and at home on the Kennet and Avon, we have been approached with a nervous hostility by people from outside the community, their bearing (be they people who live in houses, or boaters who live in marinas) debilitated by malevolent preconceptions. The result of these initially awkward encounters is invariably the same: their opinion is changed, but only of us, as we are *'not like all the rest'*. But we are like all the rest – the only difference is that in the course of a conversation, we have ceased to be part of a Brothers Grimm Unknown, and have been cleansed of our Other-ness (that nonetheless remains projected onto our friends and associates). The growing xenophobia the boat community encounters saddens us. But this exclusionary behaviour is repeated time and time again in society; the distance from each other, and from an engaged and engaging environment, compels people to behave in ways that are anything from ill-advised to downright immoral.

However, it is worth remembering that though there is a rising tide of prejudice, it should not eclipse the kind, interesting and supportive interactions that are also experienced with local canal residents and between boaters of different demographics. No community, be it on water or land, is perfect. Too often, a minority attract a disproportionate focus of attention that overshadows the positive elements of the wider picture, and these small details roll into great cycles of negativity that flow in both directions. Yet surely it would be better for attention to be focused on the obstacles that divide people rather than fuelling the division, so that together, solutions can be found to the problems that inevitably occur when a way of life, lived by many, faces new and unasked-for upheavals.

18 Ibid, p. 245
19 Ibid

* * *

"Conflict exists when there is no integration between challenge and response."

J. Krishnamurti

Sadly, we have observed a growing atmosphere of persecution in the way the waterways are governed. On 12th July 2012, just two weeks before we moved aboard our narrowboat, the newly-founded charity, Canal & River Trust, took over the guardianship of the canals and rivers of England and Wales from British Waterways, a statutory corporation owned entirely by the government of the UK. The Trust is responsible for maintaining over 2,200 miles of inland waterways that date back hundreds of years. Every year, countless locks, banks, bridges, aqueducts and much else require extensive and expensive maintenance. Raising funds and raising awareness is a task in itself, and balancing the needs of fishermen, holidaymakers, marina boaters, continuous cruisers and the estimated 18-20 million people who visit the canals every year for the tranquillity it offers, as well as the walking and cycling routes that the towpaths provide, is a most commendable juggling act. And all of this is done under threat of a substantial drop in government funding.

Though personal experience shows that there are a great many kind and intelligent people both working and volunteering for the Canal & River Trust, the Trust as a whole has repeatedly come under fire. Accusations of 'fat cat' salaries[20] and complaints about the creeping privatisation and gentrification of many parts of the network[21] (seen in the number of 14-day mooring spaces being lost in favour of property development and short-term moorings for holiday boats) are amongst the many criticisms that have been levelled. At the same time, draconian policies aimed at continuous cruisers, highlight the strong

---

20 "In 2009 the then leader of the Opposition, David Cameron, made headlines with his attack on 'fat-cats' who earned more than the Prime Minister for running taxpayer-funded bodies. Fourth on the list of those he named and shamed, at £284,000 was Robin Evans, then in charge of British Waterways, now chief executive of CRT." See Stanford, Peter. 'Canal & River Trust brings waves of discontent on the water', *The Telegraph*, 23rd July 2012. Canal & River Trust's annual report and accounts for the year to 31st March 2019 show that chief executive Richard Parry was paid £214,155 and the highest paid member of staff was Stuart Mills, chief investment officer, who received £228,992. See Preston, Rob. 'Canal & River Trust's income rises to £210m', *Civilsociety News*, 31st July 2019

21 On the 24th May 2019 the NBTA London (National Bargee Travellers Association) marched to the Canal & River Trust offices in Little Venice and on the 25th May held a flotilla protest in Paddington to demonstrate against the loss of moorings due to the gentrification and privatisation of the towpath

perception that there are policymakers within the Trust who are blind to the very real issues affecting the lives of the many people who have made a home here on the waterways.

We witnessed, both on the Kennet and Avon and on our travels around the country that, until relatively recently, the waterways' fortnightly mobility rituals, for most continuous cruisers with attachments to a place, typically covered an annual range of roughly 12 miles. It is a manageable distance if you have commitments to a place, allowing all of your needs to be met by bicycle. Movement is a much-cherished feature of the lifestyle. The difficulties only arise when being told to move too far; to places inaccessible by public transport or lacking in basic amenities such as water points and waste disposal. And this is beginning to happen.

From early on, it became apparent that the Canal & River Trust viewed the community at the western end of the Kennet and Avon as a 'problem', one that they were keen to address. In 2014 a 'neighbourhood scheme' was trialled to monitor boat movements at the western end of the canal, with a view to establishing new cruising patterns for boaters without a home mooring. Though the right to live on a boat without a home mooring is enshrined in the 1995 British Waterways Act, section 17, *Conditions as to Certificates and Licences*, stipulates that vessels must be "used bona fide for navigation" and "without remaining continuously in any one place for more than 14 days or such longer period as is reasonable in the circumstances". Throughout the course of their guardianship, the Canal & River Trust have sought to define their interpretation of *bona fide navigation* to create rules and guidelines that, if not adhered to, are backed up with threats to terminate boat licences, thereafter to even seize vessels. In effect, they would be making the boats' occupants homeless.

An atmosphere of fear and uncertainty has been generated: boaters are unsure as to exactly how far they will need to travel to comply with the latest licensing terms, as cruising patterns that had been satisfactory for over a decade are now being routinely met with restricted licences. The National Bargee Travellers Association describes Canal & River Trust's enforcement policies as "vague and inconsistently imposed" and asserts that "it uses these policies to reduce the number of full 12-month licences by restricting licences of those it considers non-compliant to six months or refusing to renew licences altogether[22]". In 2015 the Canal & River Trust spent £434,000 on legal

22 http://www.bargee-traveller.org.uk/boat-dwellers-protest-outside-canal-river-trusts-offices/

fees to evict boat dwellers[23] and in 2016 some 1,130 boaters throughout the country were threatened with eviction after their licences were restricted to less than 12 months[24]. The most recent guidelines state "that it is very unlikely that anyone travelling a range of less than 20 miles during their licence period would be able to satisfy us that they are bona fide navigating, and that normally we would expect a greater range".

Twenty miles for a child riding to school on a bicycle is a long way. Parents, together with local councils and headmasters, have made great efforts to initiate dialogues with the Trust, seeking concessions that would make school more accessible to boat children. As the Head Teacher of a local primary school said: "Because of your [Canal & River Trust's] interpretation of the law, we are spending money that is very tight to enable these children to learn. The parents are under stress and the children are exhausted because of the journey they have made to get to school[25]". The need to cover greater distances has meant that it has become increasingly difficult for the majority to manage without a motor vehicle. This is a great shame for the community and the environment, and puts additional pressure on the relationship between boaters and local residents, as the availability of parking becomes a contested issue. In 2016 boaters across the country took part in demonstrations to express their opposition to what they saw as the charity's punitive and unlawful enforcement policy[26], whilst a petition calling on the Canal & River Trust to stop enforcing on distance and movement patterns was signed by over 33,000 people[27] – all this to little or no avail. Governing the waterways in a way that imposes upon this community a constant state of needless hardship, anxiety and fear, is of no ultimate benefit to anyone.

The boating community is comprised of a great many positive and proactive human beings, who embrace their way of life and are able to make the most of a lifestyle that for many, would contain an insurmountable number of hardships. Yet their optimistic attitude should not conceal the fact that many boaters simply do not have a choice: they cannot afford a house or even a room to rent; there are very few home moorings on the Kennet and Avon and those that do become available are sold off in auction to the highest bidder,

23 http://www.bargee-traveller.org.uk/protest-at-canal-river-trust-offices-10th-may/
24 http://www.bargee-traveller.org.uk/boat-dwellers-protest-outside-canal-river-trusts-offices/
25 https://kanda.boatingcommunity.org.uk/head-teacher-condemns-crts-inhumane-enforcement-policy-in-meeting-with-mp/
26 http://www.bargee-traveller.org.uk/boat-dwellers-protest-outside-canal-river-trusts-offices/
27 http://www.londonboaters.org/bargee-travellers-march

leaving no chance or prospect to the most vulnerable. In the current climate of rising house prices and zero hours contracts, it is naïve to think that people can simply *choose another way of life*[28]. The boating community, whether it is born of necessity or an attraction to the lifestyle, is a reality with attendant consequences. Future policy should be directed towards assisting boaters, rather than reducing the numbers of boaters without a home mooring.

* * *

"It is one thing to photograph people. It is another to make others care about them by revealing the core of their humanness."

Paul Strand

When we began this book, we envisioned it as a protest, our contribution towards the safeguarding of this community that had inspired us with so much hope. We wanted to add to the comprehensive – but buried – knowledge that can quell irrational fears, and imagined that by people seeing the beauty of life on the waterways, they would come to understand that alternative forms of existence are not intrinsically a threat to them. Talk on the towpath was of collective actions, demonstrations and marches, and we hoped that these pages would, through readers' eyes, reach their hearts to inspire understanding and acceptance. But now, as the years have passed by and we have watched the story unfold, it is clear that the book will not be a chronicle of politically astute moments. Instead, it feels more like a eulogy, to a community being slowly disbanded by the uncertainties created by the ever-changing benchmarks of the Canal & River Trust, and its targeting of individuals to create a collective fear. The insistence that continuous cruisers cover greater and greater distances has brought on a new, tangibly unwelcome reality of isolation, as each person, couple or family struggles against the demands of jobs or schooling to comply with the changing criteria being imposed upon them. Day after day the people of this community are losing the battle to preserve their identity, their homes and their way of life. What is required is more than a protest. A revolution of consciousness is needed;

---

28 In 2017 there were 1.15 million households on the waiting list for social housing in England. See https://england.shelter.org.uk

people must learn to respect the non-aggressive lifestyles of others – to facilitate, not debilitate them – and to view one another for who (not what) we are: humans and beings, not stocks and bonds. It is a fact that people live on boats, go to work and have children attending school; it does not need (or ask) to be a negative fact. An important social space in a world of rising anxiety, where people can think, learn and breathe is being crushed.

By its very presence, a proactively interdependent community such as the one on the Kennet and Avon Canal, demonstrates a growing dissatisfaction with mainstream society, (as well as an increasing inability to achieve financial security within it), and though many of the struggles experienced by the canal community are unique to their environment, it is in essence a microcosm of the struggles being experienced both nationally and globally, where a market for luxury has taken precedence over concerns for humanity.

* * *

"We are all, in principle, capable of limiting our wants to our needs; the problem is that a competitive monetized economy puts us under continual pressure to want more and more."
Edward and Robert Skidelsky

In 2016, doctors in England wrote 64.7 million prescriptions for antidepressant drugs at a cost of over £266.6 million to the NHS[29]. Mental illness, violence and obesity are all on the rise, and all are symptoms of a society that, whilst finding itself at the pinnacle of both material and technological achievement, also exposes itself as being socially, spiritually and physically unwell[30]. Advertisers have colonised both private and public spaces, permeating lives with debilitating anxieties that stoke the destructive competitiveness of Western philosophy, to create a culture of mutual indifference and self-centredness, one in which the hyper-normalisation of consumer culture leaves the average person feeling alone in a crowd and crowded when alone. The UK is ranked as the fifth largest economy in the world and the fourth largest advertising market, with a projected spend

---

29 Campbell, Denis. 'NHS prescribed record number of antidepressants last year', *The Guardian*, 29th June 2017
30 Wilkinson, Richard and Pickett, Kate. *The Spirit Level: Why Greater Equality Makes Societies stronger,* (London: Bloomsbury Press, 2010), p.3

of over £26 billion by the end of 2020[31]. We believe this corporate consumer culture leaves the general public both debt-ridden and bewildered, fertile soil for its initiation into the Blame Game. It also serves to conceal the fact that the UK is ranked amongst the most unequal societies in the world[32] and has one of the worst environments for press freedom in Western Europe[33] (six billionaires own or have majority voting shares in most of the national newspapers and corporate advertising revenue regularly censors editorial content[34]). At a time of unprecedented corporate and private wealth[35] that the UK is breaking apart its welfare system[36] and threatening the NHS with privatisation, whilst failing to provide adequate recognition to its caregivers, social workers, educators and artists is a disgrace. More and more people are feeling overworked, stressed and exhausted. Is it therefore any wonder that they are looking for ways out?

* * *

"It is true that it remains unclear how to establish a viable, free, and humane post-capitalist order...But every advance in history, from ending slavery and establishing democracy to ending formal colonialism, has had to conquer the notion at some point that it was impossible to do because it had never been done before."

Noam Chomsky

Between 2010 and 2019 the world saw more mass movements demanding radical change

31 https://airoutdoor.co.uk/blog/how-many-ads-seen-one-day/

32 Suneson, Grant and Stebbins, Samuel. 'These 15 countries have the widest gaps between rich and poor', *USA Today*, 28th May 2019

33 Waterson, Jim. 'UK among the worst in western Europe for press freedom', *The Guardian*, 25th April 2018

34 Jones, Ed. 'Five reasons why we don't have a free and independent press in the UK and what we can do about it', *Open Democracy*, 18th April 2019

35 In the 12 months to summer 2018 the UK's ranks of the ultra-rich (people with fortunes of more than £38 million) swelled by 400 to nearly 5,000 as the fortunes of the already very wealthy grow at a far faster rate than the general population. See Neate, Rupert. 'Hundreds join growing rich list of Britain's ultra-rich', *The Guardian*, 18th October 2018

36 One in three billionaires in the UK have made donations to the Conservative party since 2005, and since David Cameron took power in 2010 billionaires and corporations have been given £86 billion through successive cuts to corporation tax, see Proctor, Kate. 'John McDonnell to attack £100bn tax giveaway to UK's billionaires', *The Guardian*, 18th November 2019. In the same period, real-terms funding for local authorities has been cut by 49 per cent; more than 478 libraries and 600 youth centres have been forced to close; and legal aid, benefits, police enforcement, education and social care are all suffering under lack of funding whilst the use of food banks doubled between 2013 and 2017, see Maguire, Patrick and Chakelian, Anoosh. 'The deepest cuts: austerity measured', *New Statesman*, 10th October 2018

than in any period since the Second World War[37]. Prolific thinkers are anxiously trying to draw attention to the need for positive social and environmental transformation. In 2017, the Dalai Lama released his book *A Call for Revolution* – a rallying cry to young people everywhere to take action to bring in a new era of compassion. He urges all people to cultivate a sense of interconnected vigilance towards every act of consumption[38], and to re-evaluate the way life is organised. His message is clear and expressed in no uncertain terms: "The twenty-first century will be the century of peace, or humanity will cease to be[39]".

Not long ago I was walking on the cliff tops in Cornwall, the sun was setting in a stormy sky most spectacularly over the sea and I was carrying my son, only nine months old, against my chest; the beauty of the moment was overwhelming and I had the most profound feeling that I did not want him to live in fear, fear of the filth in the sea and the pollution in the air, fear of the chemicals in our food and fear of his own helplessness in the face of it – October 2018

We believe it is up to every human being alive today to play their part in ensuring that this is not the reality for future generations. The conveniences that have been created are hard to sacrifice, yet it is our belief that, step by step, every individual can make a difference and through supportive connections with one another, connections that transcend national borders, these differences can be maintained.

A new generation is growing up keenly aware of the problems that the planet is facing, and is fuelled with the energy to make the necessary changes. It is imperative that the stories that form the foundations of their personalities are ones of hope: narratives that inspire confidence in themselves and their fellow human beings, and nurture global cooperation rather than competition. We believe that children (and adults alike) need to be taught to understand their significance as consumers and the potential power this holds to subvert consumer society and together cultivate a culture of moderation. We feel

---

37 Chenoweth, Erica; Choi-Fitzpatrick; Pressman, Jeremy; Santos, Felipe G; Ulfelder, Jay. 'The global pandemic has spawned new forms of activism - and they're flourishing', *The Guardian*, 20th April 2020
38 Dalai Lama, p. 45
39 Ibid, p. 21

there is a need for people to be encouraged to take care of what they love rather than fixate on what they don't; to replace the psychological cycles of negativity with ones of positivity and beauty. The challenges that are faced are complex, and the solutions by no means straightforward, but we think the journey can begin by asking questions such as: How much do I think is enough? What do I think a more equal society would look like? How can my surroundings be organised to cultivate a sense of purpose, belonging and pride in both where I live and in the people I live amongst? We believe that if the people of the planet pose themselves positive questions, we will all begin to move towards positive futures. Ones in which it is no longer acceptable that 67 billionaires hold as much wealth as the world's poorer half, and where together, people can bring an end to the culture of debt and depression that causes so much suffering.

For this reason, peripheral spaces such as the canal are vitally important to the future of society. The canal not only provides an affordable place to live, it generates a multiplicity of community centres; spaces where important social, economic and political remedies can be created and exchanged. That canals are far enough from the frenetic pace of mainstream society, where the burden of meeting one's basic needs habitually eclipses any opportunity to reflect upon, let alone mitigate that burden, is hardly a coincidence in this respect. In our years on the canal we have encountered the greatest concentration so far, of people who embody the philosophy of global change through personal development. For many on the canal, sustainable consumption is an ethical application, not simply a topic of conversation. Their diversity of knowledge and approaches to societal and environmental concerns have been an inspiration to us. Some are committed to improving the sustainability of cities through methods such as aquaponics and clean energy solutions; others are working with children from some of the most troubled backgrounds to restore their self-esteem through positive interaction with the natural world. Whatever their approach may be, people living on the canal are concerned, they are creative, they are thinking and they are communicating; and we believe that only in environments where *time* is a valued and nurtured asset, will new ideas be incubated that can help solve the problems the planet is facing. We understand that by its very essence a community such as this will be viewed with suspicion, its fluid decentralised horizontalism posing too much of a threat to the current established order. But we see the established order as already under threat from its own greed and corruption: it is from spaces and communities such as these that positive alternative futures will be imagined.

It is the *people* that make a community; not the type of dwelling they inhabit. The fundamental principles of valuing time over money, respecting nature over consumption, prioritising conversation with neighbours over screen time and inclusivity over gated communities, can be replicated in any environment. While difference exists, and the desire for it continues, the proliferation of spaces in which creativity and independent thought can flourish should be celebrated and encouraged, not shut down.

* * *

"It is not a finished Utopia that we ought to desire, but a world where imagination and hope are alive and active."

Bertrand Russell

"...Atticus, he was real nice."...

"Most people are Scout, when you finally see them."

Harper Lee

Tom, Mazy, Mops and Stevie

We're the kind of people who see a railway carriage or whatever and say, 'I could live in that', whereas I've never really had that feeling with houses. Before the boat we'd been travelling overland in a double-decker bus as part of the band in a traveling circus, that took us from England to Bangladesh. We had friends who lived on the canal in Bath, it was always a nice place to be, and on our return it seemed like the obvious choice to make. There were only a few boats on the canal back in those days and it was a very unusual thing to do. That was back in 2004.

We had managed to save some money so we had the boat built; it was just a lined sailaway because that was all we could afford. Inside it had the engine, the portholes and the windows, and it was spray foamed and lined with marine ply, but it was just a huge space with no rooms. Tom had just been born and Mazy was four. We'd spent all our money so we lived in a dome-tent at one end, which is now our bedroom. We had a piano and the Rayburn and that was it.

When the canals were run by British Waterways we didn't have to move much, well at least not so far, we still had to move every two weeks, but it was all really relaxed. Back then people were not really aware of the canals. There weren't very many boats around and there were very few hire boats. I suppose once they became a charity, that's when they started making up all these rules. That's when the recommended distances began to rise. First of all it was around 17km, then 17km turned into 20km, and then it was 20 miles and then 20 miles with expectations of considerably more.

We got our first restricted licence (a licence limited to six months rather than 12) after CRT reviewed our 2017 to 2018 cruising pattern. At this time the recommended distance was between 15 and 20 miles and we had done 17 and a half. We'd done the distance and had all the photos to prove it. So in the six-month period of our next licence we did 13 miles; we didn't do what you have to do in 12 months that's for sure, because it's a six-month licence. We were always asking them "how far are we supposed to go?" but they would never tell us. It turns out they're not allowed to tell us how far we're supposed to go in six months, but we didn't know that at the time and we had to guess. After six months they said they were still not satisfied with our cruising pattern so they gave us a second restricted licence. This time we did more then 17 miles. It was after this that they told us that we were already on the naughty step and now we had to leave their waters.

We were given a Section 8 and told to remove our vessel from their waters, or get a home mooring. It was threatening. It gave us a month or they would take us to court and potentially take our home. Yet they still never really specified what displeased them, just that they were not satisfied with our cruising pattern.

It didn't matter to them that this had been our home for over 14 years, that it was our community and our chosen lifestyle. It didn't matter at all that we had a family, that the children were raised here, that Mazy won a scholarship to the Royal High School and Tom is a brilliant musician. It didn't matter that we worked locally, that we've always paid our licence on time or that there were no available home moorings in the Bath area. Whatever we said, however nice our letters were, it just didn't seem to make any difference at all. It's the first time I've ever come up against anything like this. It was stressful. Mazy and Tom were finding it very difficult because all their mates are in Bath, and they went to school in Bath, so of course the further away we had to go the more inconvenient it got. What I find really puzzling is why we have to move so far? What's the point in going halfway to Bristol taking a photo and turning around and going to Devizes? It's just completely pointless. I mean, okay, let's move every two weeks, but at present it just means everyone shuffles around and burns diesel; some days I'd be driving for nearly three hours just doing school runs, yet CRT couldn't care less.

We felt very much singled out and picked on. It felt like they needed to prove a point, so they took someone who had been on the canal a long time (and who everyone knows tries to do the distance) and they decided to throw everything at us. There's a lot of uncertainty regarding what constitutes 'continuously cruising' and whether they are allowed to evict you from the canal, so it would have been a bit of a pivotal case. We took legal advice and even though we felt we were in the right – we'd done the distance and had all the photos to prove it – we realised that we couldn't go to court because we just couldn't afford to. They could out-resource us completely; they had a QC who was an expert in Inland Waterways Law and they could easily have chucked a couple of hundred thousand at it, and we wouldn't have stood a chance. We had so much to lose, I mean they haven't, it's not their homes is it? But if they'd won and we had had to match they're expenditure we'd have had to sell the boat, and the rest, to pay back the loan and they know this. They know they've got us trapped when it comes to finances and that's just too stressful.

So in the end we had to run off to Bristol (to waters independent of CRT). We were fortunate to have friends who helped us get a mooring in the centre, but that's what happened, they just pursued us and kept threatening us until we had to leave. That's when we realised they don't care about us as people or as a community. It's us that care because it's our environment. We're trying to make it a better place because it's our home, but they don't care. We're not constantly cruising anymore because we were forced to take this mooring. It's an expenditure that we could have done without, and it's difficult being stuck in Bristol when everything we do is set up in Bath. Should it have been so hard? I do fear its only going to get worse for this community, which makes it difficult not to sort of really dislike the way the canals are being governed.

Liveaboards are what really make this canal special for us. I love the people that have been attracted to the canal life; they're amazing, very creative and friendly, sometimes strange, but always accepting. I can't believe my luck mostly. It's this uniqueness and individuality in people that make the world a more beautiful and colourful place. The countryside is beautiful, but I think it's the people that make it. I'm really pleased and proud of being able to give my kids this upbringing, surrounded by good, vibrant people in a very positive community. I never felt scared for them on the canal no matter what the time. A lot of having a happy life depends on you're neighbours, doesn't it? It's so nice, it's a real special thing, and everyone is so supportive; and maybe because there's a sense of being persecuted by CRT we've become even more tightly knit as a community, because we're all sort of in it together.

– Stevie

To all the people who inhabit, for however short or long, these waterways and who made this time in our lives so special. Many people have come and gone, many friendships were made, some for a day, some for a lifetime.

Thank you

What does the canal mean to me? It is my home. It is the peaceful place of my imagination. It is where my son was born. It is the opportunity to live a life of creativity and the possibility to spend every day with my husband and my child. It is all of this and more, more than the world of my imaginings. It is a unique reality reinforced by the multitude of characters that live within it.

I have always thought myself to be a rather shy person. I have never found it easy to feel comfortable in a group, yet here on the canal, amongst so many open-hearted and open-minded individuals, I feel very much at ease. In this place I have been shown so much kindness, so much generosity. I have listened to wonderful tales of adventure and been swept away by magical dreams. Here, amongst friends, I can laugh at the silliest of things and share the deepest of thoughts. In a world such as this is it any wonder that almost a decade has slipped by in the blink of an eye?

Will I always live here? Almost certainly not. The impermanence of everything is the lens through which its beauty is focused. But whether that day will come in one year or 10 remains to be seen. At times I yearn for the golden light of India or the clarity of the Himalayas but am I yearning for memories or making plans for the future? Whichever it may be I continue to stay because right here, right now, this is the most perfect present.

– Louise

ACKNOWLEDGEMENTS

Our warmest thanks go to our family and friends who have helped turn this idea into a reality. For the roofs over our heads as we printed our photogrphs, and the words of encouragment when the end seemed out of sight; for the enthusiasm shared, and the patience shown, as we learnt to capture the world we saw with our cameras; for the tireless proofreading and guidance with design, we are wholeheartedly grateful.

Andrew, Margaret, Simon, Shu, Sue, Indra, Dot, Mike, Ben, Jay, Simone, Luca, Lief, Dru, Guy, Laura, Amy, Wendy, Tom, Will, Kim and all of the team at Photofusion, Mary, Jo, Adam, Kiu, Rob, Dan, John, Chris, Laura, Boz, Ross and Michael, you have been wonderful.

All of the photographs in this book have been captured on film and printed, by ourselves, in an analogue darkroom, prior to scanning for publication.

For print enquiries please visit:
www.sebastienandlouise.com

A Wanderings Publication
First published 2020

© Sebastien & Louise Tickner, 2020

Printed in the UK by Park Communications Ltd., London

www.wanderingspublications.com

ISBN 978-1-8381415-0-9